your knowledge of literature that you so generously shared with me inspired me to write from an early age. i am blessed to have such a sincere man as a father. no amount of words will suffice in describing how extraordinary of a person you are. i hope every daughter has a father like you. from a farmer and aspiring attorney in punjab, india to a successful businessman in america; you are the true definition of the american dream. i will forever be thankful for the way you raised big brother and i. all of my writing work is dedicated to you, and forever will be.
i am who i am today because of you.
our angel
iqbal singh samra
march 8, 1955- august 15, 2019

*

to mom and my big brother nav,

thank you for always pushing me to be my best. my beautiful mother is the most courageous, heroic, loving and hard working woman i know; instilling in me the power of education and compassion, you are forever my best friend. nav, you have always encouraged me to be strong and independent. constantly believing in me and my craft even when i didn't believe in myself. i've looked up to you for as long as i can remember. thank you for being the best big brother any little sister could ask for.

priyanka samra

table of contents

inside the mind's attic

she wrote her mental fireworks
on dollar store napkins
with a flimsy .50 cent pencil
hoping they will
one day
resonate with minds
in all corners of the world
even with little girl
in the slums of india
whose only escape from poverty
lies in the magic of books

the girl in 205

it is
the type of mental pain
that glues my eyes shut in the mornings
apathetic of the outside world
basking in melancholy
time slowly peeled the layers
of my agony away
and relished my core wound
with sweet honey
my awakening
has the world always
presented me
with so many possibilities
has mother earth always been
this beautiful
was the color magenta
always this captivatingly
stunning
has oxygen always
tasted this delicious
the adrenaline to fulfill
my purpose and dreams
is electrifying
everyday
started smelling like
the comfort of
my favorite candle
sweet apple cinnamon
utterly euphoric

bittersweet epiphany

here you are
gallantly diving deep
into the ridges and folds
of my brain
unwrapping my thoughts
enamored by their beauty
starry eyed
you eternally swim
deeper and deeper
an unquenchable
infatuation
with my mind

olympic dives

her unclipped wings shatter glass ceiling dreams
a heart to pursue divergent ideas
and express indiscriminate compassion
lifting up adversaries and allies
radiating truth over gloss
an anomaly in a conformist society

the revolutionary

they hired the best carpenter
in all the land
to sand down her edges
adamantly
they grew back sharper
they found a top surgeon
in all the land
to cut her wings
stubbornly
they grew back larger
let her embody her inimitable aura
free of a premade mold

tenacious anatomy

i know it is hard
but you are a sword
my dear
once the pain elapses
you will be restored
into the most indestructible woman
on this earth
you are a warrior
under construction
be patient

formation

to make art is the open up your insides
to judgment
to open the backside of your minds closet
to vulnerability
that is the beauty
the liberation of painting your own paradise

in the pursuit of art

some nights
the pain will
wake you at 2am
to make your ears bleed

painfully early

if you let
their words cut your eyes
you will be blind
to the things you once
loved about myself
your heart will sink
when their words
bulldoze the gates
to your mind
again and again
the words will punch you
in the brain
the words that
had once so effortlessly
escaped their lips
in seconds
resist the
initial incision

a lethal weapon

we cannot rebuild
into the best version
of ourselves
until we are broken
again
and again
and again
if we accept our pain
we learn
until we flourish
if we negate our pain
we suffer
until we deteriorate
the prerequisite of growth
is pain
the key
is acceptance

a bittersweet gift

an intoxicating smirk
complimented her sparking eyes
where within
there is incurable grief
mentally scattered
each thought zealously escaping her brain
in the sweltering water she lay in
relieved to be out of mental captivity
blood red dior stained her swarovski glass
one last exhale of relief
before drowning in her blue moon diamonds
at 3am

monetary misery

real gold
is seen in eyes
of the lives you have touched
it is heard in the ears
of the deaf
it is felt in the bodies
of those who are paralyzed

the power of gold

by the time we realize
the beauty of the lemon tree
in our backyard
the fruits will have perished

the auspicious tree

as the years pass
the pair of eyes fixate
on the sand traveling down
the neck of the hourglass
the gradual becoming
of a blinkered horse

peripheral universe atrophy

how do you fail to dignify
the very women
whose hips cracked to give life
to kings and queens?

mothers

one neuron ignites the next
proliferating into a mental wildfire
birthing imprisonment
or emancipation

cerebral electricity

the yellow tape that wrapped around
her hips every month
now felt like a snake
slithering up
from her 34 inch emaciated hips to her neck
wrapping tighter and tighter
it was time for her monthly suffocation
she looked in the mirror
unable to recognize the stranger
living deep in the ocean of her blue eyes
dying a little inside in convincing herself
that she was alright
but the numbers dropping
on the tape measure each month
said otherwise
the numbers that made her boss smirk
as if he had just won the lottery
a slimmer waist
put more money in his pocket
but one little problem
he pulled out a black marker
prompting her heart to drop
he circled her 'problem areas'
"only two weeks to fashion week"
he soullessly said
then gave her
the 'drop the weight
or to hell with you' look

34-24-34

one day
when your sacrifices
and your parent's sacrifices
and their parent's sacrifices
have grown gardens
of fruits and vegetables
bring in all the chairs
and decorate the table nice

a meal for all

i break bread with the impoverished
because underneath their torn coats
so many are innocent gold
in a world of guilty gold

the affluence of the poor

you dove into the deep end
when you knew
you could not swim
then when i saved you
you championed
your own strong arms

impetuous nose dives into my soul

i unlock the lock of the closet
in the deepest corner of your mind
pull out your subconscious
and paint it into my words
then gently tuck it back into it's nest

spilling your secrets

only when she left him
was she able to
smell the mid summer
sweet peas blossom
once again
taste gingerbread
on christmas eve
once again
hear the marvelous
sound of für elise
once again

resurrection of the senses

words are the most powerful tool
in the universe
use them rashly
and a king could become a vagrant
use them wisely
and a vagrant could become a king

a double-edged sword

and alas
when the dark horse is a star
glistening in the night sky
they will be watching
from their castles up high
with the same
haughty eyes

the village girl

dear,
do not forget
your most vital
formless vitamin
a capsule
packed with
self love
resilience
confidence
and integrity

your daily dose

he knocked
and he knocked
and he knocked
he pounded his fist on my door
finally
i opened that door
his persistence
had my heart
heart held in my hands
before i could gently hand it over
he reached over
with that irresistible
charming smile
snatched my heart
and dropped it into his jar
of hearts
and then
closed the lid
tighter than
those damn
strawberry jam jars

jar of hearts

when instigating a downfall
satisfies your eyes
like shooting stars
in the night sky
then remember
when you see her
rising back up from the horizon
that there is nothing in this world
quite as destructible
as the fire you created
inside her soul

a california wildfire

you summoned the darkest clouds above my head
in privacy
and when they were watching
you put a coat on my back
and you showcased your devious smile
when they left
you yanked the coat off my back
and looked at me
with the most belittling eyes
it became the most frigid night
you went around town
to boast about
how great of a heart
rests in your chest
when what rests inside
is in fact
rotten

behind your 32 teeth

each year
we are given one or two pieces
when we finally fit one of the last pieces
to complete our masterpiece
we notice a few pieces have gone missing
or are taken away from us
the more we dwell on the missing pieces
the less time we have
searching for the rest of the pieces
our masterpiece may never be complete
but that is good
we are on a constant hunt
to find the pieces
which allows us to
perpetually grow on all levels
what would life be
once the masterpiece is complete
perfect indeed
but dreary

the imperfect puzzle

ayesha does not have much
she dreams of building herself
a beautiful door
but she has no money
she heads out to the woods
and brings back a piece of wood
she examines it and wonders how she will possibly
build a beautiful door
there are twigs sticking out in all directions
one edge is perfectly square
another rectangular
the other triangular
she goes to the drawing board to map out
the perfect door
she fails multiple times
at this point
she wants to give up
she is out of ideas
and motivation
but then
she thinks what was the point
of coming all this way
if she was going to give up
so she went back to the drawing board
carefully choosing every hinge and bolt
sanding and carving away
day after day
year after year
until finally
the door was finished
but then in an earthquake
her creation is destroyed
fortunately
she has the skills to rebuild from scratch

…on the other hand
a father
hands his daughter jen a beautiful door
in it's impeccable nature
painted
and glossed
to perfection
for jen
it is as easy as attaching the door
to the entry way
so she does
the door is flawed
so she goes to the shop
to buy tools to build a new one
she buys the most expensive tools
in the shop
thinking that they will build
the most durable beautiful door
she goes home with her tools
but does not know
where to start

handmade doors

he threw his trusty bright whites at me
from across the room
but his dark eyes screamed
'i can't wait to destroy this one next'

the crystal clear deceit

and when i finally put an end to us
there was still hope
that you would come back
with a bouquet of my favorite lilies
and an apology
on one of those pretty
hallmark cards

false hopes

you turned them upside down
and watched their eyes bleed
while you threw back shots
and ate wagyu meat
then gathered your
friends around the table
and gave them a front row seat

tickets to the show

home is
within the unbounded walls of my mind
home is
within each organ
each cell
and each atom of my body
home cannot be found
in other people
that is their home

the galaxies in my blood

congratulations
at last
you have won her over
the years of admiring her
and soaking her in
in absolute awe
and mustering up
the courage to ask her
to hold your hand forever
in this roller coaster of a life
but now that you have her
never forget to
eternally chase her
inebriating mystic
the very thing
that drew your eyes to her
when you first saw her
in that little brick coffee shop
behind her laptop
and thick framed glasses
lost in spilling her thoughts
out onto paper

her

how electrified my spirit felt
when i rested my head
on your iron chest
but i knew it was a wrap
especially when
i felt
your soul escape
your body
there it went
like smoke hurriedly running
from a flame
into the air
into the abyss

you are free to go

she was different
far more different
than the different ones
the kind that
he wrote about
in his journal every night
before dozing off into dream land
to see her
she was also
the one he broke
over
and over again
only when she left
did he realize
how special she was
that is when
he put pen to paper
to write about her
every night

the one who got away

why would i
put up with anyone
who tries to
feed my mind
my *home*
dirt
if my home
is not being fed
anything less
than the best fruits
in all of the land
my brain does not want to eat

brain fruit

they buried her alive
with grins on their faces
the size of texas
but her ambiance
quivered the soil
the elevated her up
burial after burial
breaking the heavily packed
layers and layers
of dirt they piled onto her

unperturbed spirit

leaves rupture into ruby reds
a tulip bashfully recoils
bees reconcile
the stars watch you a little longer
the days are warm no longer

autumn in oregon

as soon as i set my feet
on the sand
the moist mist
hugs my face
the deep blue
waves pull me in
seducing me
to come closer
the sand below
transforms from a firm clay
into slushy mud
the seaweed washed up on shore
intertwines between my toes
firing a chill up my spine
i shake off the seaweed
and head closer
the cold water
wraps itself around my feet
like holiday wrapping paper
in that moment
a rejuvenating satisfaction
i crave when i am away
from the sea
the sea
is music
to my inner scorpion

the sea

the sun peaks through the blinds
knocking
to see if i am up
i open one eye
and hesitate to open the other
afraid of the rays
stinging my eyes
i get up
and stretch
straightening my spine
extending my arms
to open up my body
i turn my face towards the sun
and it warmly welcomes me
to another beautiful day

saturday mornings

thank you
for your snowy mountains
that gift my eyes pristine scenery
your cascading waterfalls
that gift my body water
for my protection and nourishment
your trees
that gift me air
for the movement of my breath
and circulation
your various plants
that gift me nutrients to perform
for fire
that gifts me light and heat
for space
that gifts my body growth and change
between my cells my breath
and my thoughts

dear mother earth

it is when the first page whole heartedly
captivates every cell
in my body
that i know this will be a good one
each page is turned with a more
heightened sense of anticipation
than the previous
my eyes cannot wait to
jump to the next line
until i reach
the last word in the book
i have fed my mind
a tumultuous ride

a mental outing

taking two subways
and two taxis
to get to the pretty glass skyscraper
in soho
i was twenty two
bright eyed
waiting in line for hours
along with hundreds of others
in the stilettos i was given
two sizes too small
four hours of
hoping and wishing
for an old man
to shatter me with these words
"sorry, we already have one brown girl in our show"
commenting my frail figure
*"you may want to slim down on those hips, after all it is fashion week
castings honey"*
you gave me a gift
the gift of realization
that i want no part
of this darkness
i want no part of a world
that throws the precious minds
of young women into washing machines
full of toxic detergent

human mannequin misery

every time i feel like my hands
are about to grasp you
to toss you out of my mind
you swim ahead faster
then glance back
to watch me struggle
you chuckle a little
and continue
cruising forward
with such ease

relishing pain with rainbow sprinkles

she was the type to
build sand castles in monsoon season
dive into the ocean in a thunderstorm
wash darkness out of the night
send water back into the raincloud
and run a marathon on black ice

the woman in red

cruising through
the cosmic chaos
trying to swim out of
it's marvelous mayhem
year after year
all while
the sand in the hourglass
diminishes

the clock thaws

i love the kind of mornings
when
i melt into my sheets
my blanket hugs
the hills and dips of my body
like snow cuddling a mountain tightly
but not too tight
just enough
so my blanket feels like
my nest
tucked away from the chaotic
world on the other side
of my blanket

a feather cocoon

when i sit on the floor
i melt into the earth
i become a part of the earth
i am one with the earth
a beam of light
shines from beneath the soil
up my spine
out of my brain
and connects
with the supreme power
above

chakras

beautiful lady
he had thrown
your heart
onto hot coils
and watched it sauté
yet still
here you are
waiting on that black widow
to metamorphose into a butterfly
you have forgotten that
you are a work of art
who should be adored
with a pair of eyes
full of nothing
but awe

wake up, dear

she is much more beautiful
when you
start seeing the parts of her
that eyes cannot see
you have only seen
the tide pools
when there is an entire ocean
her waves will
pull you back
and down
and sideways
but if you keep swimming
you will discover
a beauty that
could even make
a diamond turn green
with envy

mariana trench

formal education
teaches us
how to crack an egg
it is up to us
to pour it into the frying pan
and cook
our best
most nutritious omelet
or scrambled egg
to feed ourselves
and those around us
especially those who do not have
the hands to cook

cooking for others

empowerment
is craving the knowledge
to build my psyche
taller than towers
stretching their hands
to caress the clouds
it is to extend the arms of my mind
past the succulent clouds
to reach for the galaxies
that we yet
know nothing of

a millennial's liberation

to the man of your dreams
your soul will shine
like auroras in the night sky

your striking sparkle

the creator gifts us a film
but no remote
we waste our lives
trying to figure out how
to rewind
or fast forward
rather than relishing the film
as it unfolds

screenplays written by god

sometimes our most remarkable rise
comes cloaked in a parcel
wrapped in the darkest paper
of woe

gift wrap

time halts
when you drop everyone off
the corners of the earth
in your divine exchange of words
with her
the gloom of apathy
breaks apart to reveal
the sunshine of july
and your eyes sparkle like sirius

her medicine

your mental sea
of self-worth is often cooked
using the ingredients
of their words
do not let a sour droplet
mushroom in the ocean
of sweet honey

the inner sea

pull out the treasure chest
hidden under your tongue
unlock your words
and paint them on the walls
in bold red

the valiant goddess

death is the blossoming
of the soul's lungs
it is the inception
of it's everlasting liberation

the commencement

the lines at the corner of each eye
deepening when you laugh
the blemishes imperfectly placed
darkening in the california sun
to tear troughs that symbolize
your power through
the darkest times in life
collectively and magnificently
paint the most beautiful face
one that no photograph
will do justice to
but
one that the raw human eye
only will

old and beautiful

solace is found
on frequent deep sea dives
into the third eye
of my inner universe
unhindered by societal noise
swimming further and deeper
a liberating outing
for my soul

night swims under the stars

my paint brush introduces itself
to the canvas reluctantly
i hesitate to pinpoint
where
the first stroke
will engrave itself
the first brush of color
is so permanent
so i have to be careful
there
it is too far right
here
it is too far left
now overthinking
i turn my mind on mute
and i flick my wrist
in the most
blissful liberation
and
before i know it
the strokes collectively
create the best piece
i have ever painted

unconstrained

a brain in poverty
and a body in poverty
are a world of a difference
a brain in poverty
could belong in a body that lives
in a world of riches
a brain in poverty
always sees the glass
as half empty
it does not reach down
to lift anyone up
it walks over people
to get ahead
a brain in poverty
pays it's
mental mortgage
but it's house is
not a home
it exudes
hatred and gluttony
a body in poverty
could have a brain in the riches
it always sees the glass as half full
it lifts people up
it loves indiscriminately
and imminently

the power of the mind

you swiped
my mental credit card
and did not pay the bills
when i realized
how costly
each swipe
was becoming to my mind
i took
my credit card back
and now
the collection letters
come to your house
every month

do not return to sender

when i was a little girl
they told me
that my dreams
were far too big for a girl
like me
that i would see
nothing past the wooden fences
that surrounded
the oregon cottage
i grew up in
from them on
i set my sight
on chasing the sunset
on the other side
of the fence
their faces grew beat red
when they saw that
i kept going
and going
and going
until all they saw
was my long brown hair
vanishing
into my dream world

the untamed raven locks

you design a box
to your liking
and paint the four walls
with careful thought put into
each color
and each brush
then place your child
in that box from birth onward
when they go out
into the world on their own
your now adult child
can only see the four walls
that you had painted
by placing them in your
flawlessly created box
you have given them
your eyes
depriving them
of the opportunity
to develop
their own sight

a mind in packing peanuts

unearthing the mind
is like
entering an enigmatic cave
we are welcomed
unpleasantly
with a cold breeze
then we step
into an icy puddle
and sharp rocks
but then we feel
a comforting warm breeze
and we see a little light
as we walk closer
the light illuminates
our path
and we discover
the unmatched beauty

the pursuit of cerebral buttercream icing

the rain drops patter down
on the window
as if politely asking
if they may come in
i turn back to my book
reading
but not really reading
i peer over the words
to see when my coffee will arrive
a lady walks in shaking her umbrella
like a wet dog
an elderly couple
basking in nostalgia
as they discuss their
golden years back in the 50s
a college kid stressed over exams
i get lost in people watching
i zone out
and when i realize i am zoning out
snapping out of it does not sound appealing
it feels kind of nice
really nice
because
time halts
for a bit
in the little coffee shop
on 155 E 52nd St
tucked away
in the city that never sleeps

somewhere but nowhere

a heart shaped
cappuccino
is placed on my table
with a pair of
handsome hands
the kind of hands
that could chop down a tree
but
soft enough
to brush my problems
behind my ear
he notices that i am reading rumi
and before even asking my name
he asks
what my favorite piece is
and if i like james joyce
in that moment
i knew this one
would stay for a little while
maybe even
forever

the man at the coffee shop

i look forward
to the nights
i grab a pair
of my sharpest scissors
from the drawer
and
cut all ties
with the outside world
and then
tighten the ties
that stitch my brain
together so tight
that they freely release
the beauty
from one hemisphere
to the other
one thought fires
then the next
then the next
creating
cerebral fireworks
in the night sky
of the brain

evenings

a mental pandemonium
seconds before
stepping onto my home plate
a deep breath
before i recite my lines
one last time
my nerves sit
ceremoniously
i always count one two
since i was two
before my first step
onto the stage
the lights electrify my insides
and the audience
makes my soul dance

theater kid

they will blindfold
her audacious eyes
tie her exceptionally
strong tall and beautiful wings
behind her back
in order to morph them
to look like the others
and whisper gently in her ears
before stuffing them with cotton
that her abode is now
behind the rusty iron bars
in which she will fly around in
then kiss her
in the middle of her forehead
corrupting her third eye

atrophy in the aviary

the large crystal glass doors
on 6th avenue
were like flames
to my 16 year old inner moth
hatred of my body
grew like a wildfire
as if my measurements
were all i had to offer
but right before i became numb
i dove into the deep end
of salvation
to put out the flames
but my heart ached
to think
that so many girls do not feel
the raging fire engulfing
their being
lighting the path
to their destruction

a perfect lie

you go back to your hiding place
to illuminate the far east
but before you vanish
i look up
cotton candy
and sometimes
orange pineapple
with a little bit
of strawberry
i look down
light glossing over
the crashing waves
you give my eyes
these gifts
eagerly anticipating
a night on the beach
but a little sad
that you are leaving
for the day
so i close my eyes
to enjoy the last bit of warmth
on my face
as it slowly fades

california summers

watching the steam
escape the cup
i can almost
feel the glass
pressed up
against my lips
then the warm liquid
traveling
down my esophagus
turning on each muscle
awakening my body
bitter
has never been so sweet to me
the liquid
voyages through
each vein
rejuvenating
each cell
it reaches my feet
now
they are ready

morning coffee

the light
bounces off the water
crafting those
divine aquatic crystals
hesitant of the cold needles
numbing my body
but
i daringly
dive right in
within seconds
the frigid needles
turn into
a comforting cool
bodily refreshment
from the bottom
i look up
the sun
casting it's rays
on the surface
i am behind the curtain
watching the sun
work it's magic

midday swims

we go through our lives
year after year
with our eyes closed
only once we have departed
our bodily garment
and gone to the astral world
is our third eye opened
prying this eye open
while we are still breathing
the air of the earth
only comes when
we shave off the branches
and pluck the seeds
society has planted
in our brain
deep sea diving
miles and miles
into our mind
having the stamina
to continue swimming
turning the world
on mute

the inner cosmos

the city that never sleeps
in fact sleeps
with one eye open
before it opens the other
i walk down to the café
to get my vanilla latte
on 44th and 3rd
there is
the chrysler building
there it stands
tall and grand
captivating the dawn sky
with it's nearly blinding
bright lights
i feel
a refreshing mist
i see
empty yellow cabs
waiting for the clock to strike 8am
when the streets will flood with
corporate america
the streets look glossy
it rained
the night before

5am in new york city

and when i am
wholly
or even partially
shattered
i embark on the journey
of artistry
my brain paints like
it has never painted before
an innovative expedition
the pain spills out
onto the pages
a mental chaos
that somehow
exudes order
it hurts
but its also
nice
sometimes i find home
in being broken
as pain
is the key ingredient
in the recipe of
creativity

life of an artist

untied
from the knots
of society
it is like running
with my laces open
i am free to run
wherever i wish
as fast as i wish
but there is
the risk of tripping
on my laces
most
tie their laces
few
run with them
untied

shoe laces

momentarily
no where
but
heading somewhere
far from home
high above the clouds
i think
is this what heaven is like?
the pristine
white
cottony
blankets
nourishing mother earth
suddenly my problems
seem so
micro sized
and then
as we ascend
further and further up
they evaporate
i am a nomad

airplanes

i see your heart racing
faster than a race horse
competing
in the kentucky derby
your gestures
beautifully out of control
as if passionately
reciting shakespeare
under the lights
your smile brighter
than stars
in the night sky
your cheeks more red
than strawberries
in the middle
of july
your eyes on a wild safari
enamored by how
your aura dances
when you talk about
the things you love
the most

more of this

we talk about everything
under the sun
from now
until 4am
your laugh so grand
that i can
count all your teeth
heads up to
the heavens
and hysterical claps
but also
a cloud
of wistfulness
rolls in above us
tears pour down your face
you take your beautiful
sun-kissed hands
and wipe the tears
off your
summer freckles

catching up

oh and here you are again
bittersweet acquaintance
excitedly
i walk down
the college halls
and i feel as if i am
back at school
rushing from
the dining hall
to chemistry class
the tiny rooms
where we studied
until 2am
but
i look inside
and i don't see myself
i look around and i see
the faces of strangers
not my friends
a cloud of sorrow
and suddenly
i am gasping for air

nostalgia

a fear of the unknown
turns into
a ravenous hunger
to eat
the colors
to hear
the flavors
to smell
the garments
and
to touch
the foreign air
i am a sponge
zealously soaking in
the new land

travels

i throw my arms
around you
i can feel the strings
of our hearts
pulling us closer
as if they were never
meant to be separated
your soul
electrifies mine
our hearts empty out
their handsome guts
in the duration
of this exchange
time freezes
we have severed
all ties
with the outside world
to savor this very moment

hugs

i push the pedal
to thrust forward
the ocean breeze
throwing my long hair
onto my back
then airborne
flowing in the ocean mist
candidly
i feel the crunchiness
of the sand on the bike trail
as it sizzles in the august heat
the palm trees lined up
some large
some small
and all placed
disorderly
i see the rough looking graffiti
promoting world peace
and an old man with arthritis
selling hand made jewelry
the mouth watering
smell of garlic fries
and crispy sweet churros
a beautiful mayhem
the chaos relents
as i travel south
on the way
to marina del rey

saturday bike rides

left to right
back left to write
as my pen strokes move across the page
i dive into the abyss of
my cerebral universe
then suddenly
the aroma of sweet and spicy cinnamon
make me smile ear to ear
widening my eyes
i hear footsteps growing louder
accompanied by rattling glass
my door opens slowly
and i am greeted by your precious
heartwarming smile
the cups filled to the top
nearly spilling over
you carefully place the tray
on my desk as i look over my notebook
and realize how fortunate of a daughter
i am to have a father like you
i close my notebook as you
bring over my cup
before taking a sip of your own
you ask me if the sugar
in my cup is alright
and if i would like any snacks

rainy california evenings

alas
you are free from your suit
eternally liberated
to roam the planet
and other galaxies
you have given up
your bodily dress
free of any constrictions
your immortal soul
can now flourish
infinitely

the garment

our hearts shatter
when we lose the ones
we love
but
what are we really losing
but a body?
the souls that have
departed the earth
are children of god
and forever will be
they are free from
the baggage of bones
and worries
unhindered by their
bodily suit
summoned by the creator
it is not an end
it is one step
towards our relationship with those
we love the most
those we love
for eternity

the omnipresent soul

a mercenary eats all the fruits
of his trees
birthing gluttony
the key ingredient
in the malady
of mind and body

greed

audacity is gifted by the creator
to those who recognize
that they
in fact
have backbones of steel

the inner lioness

although my eyes bleed
you are eternally free
from your garment
one that
we will all flee

roam free but visit me often

they must see their plates
overflow
with plenty of sides
collecting the meager bits
from the plates of
the commoners
to pile their plates up high

dinner with the oligarchs

before you inhale
their toxic words
hold your breath
and grasp the words firmly
drop them into a jar
only retrieving them
to sprinkle onto
the fire you have been
creating in silence
then watch the flames
erupt
and break through
the glass ceiling
they said
you would never shatter

sweet venom

you pull your heart
by the roots ground in place
since you were 22 days
and place it in their palms
hoping they won't clench
this time

proceed with caution

we are all different types
of leaves
but grow from the same
roots
seeded and watered by
the impartial hands
of the creator

the human race

the seed that sprouted in the far east

as a little girl
she did not dream of being gifted with gold
on her wedding day
rather
she dreamt bursting out of her pre molded
cultural cocoon and soaring over the universe
to develop an intellectually inquisitive mind
to have an infinitely loving soul
lighting the way
even in her darkest hour

gold pleated wings

once a joyful little girl
skipping to the market
she looked up
her chocolate brown eyes
gazed at the billboard
plastered over the shop
a fair skinned model
advertising coca cola
she felt her heart sink
breaking her confidence
in her striking chocolate skin
but the billboards
that screamed
light skin privilege
in the land of melanin
did not matter
because
one day
when was all grown up
she held the highest seat
in the entire nation
her dusky skin lit the way
she became a revolutionary

children of india

the little girl roamed the streets of her village
trying to find a home
looking up at the bazaars and chaiwalas
a nomad
ripped out of her mother's comforting arms
she wanted a mother
to hush her when she cried
to teach her her first words
to buy her dolls from the shop
to hold her hand on her first day of school
most of all
she wanted to be adored
and showered with love
just like the boys

a national crisis: indias 'unwanted girls'

dear mom and dad,
you are not only my kings
you are also my best friends
my teachers and my mentors
from the days you cradled me
in your arms
you have radiated and fed my heart
kindness
warmth
and compassion
as a little girl
you taught me to go to war
if i have to
in order to fulfill my dreams
as a grown woman
you continue to instill
in me that there is no obstacle
that i cannot overcome
thank you
for giving me life

muumi and papa

the strong
warm hands
that held me at 2 minutes young
the hands that i held tightly
everyday to and from school
to save me from slipping on the
cold canadian ice
the hands that
when placed on my dark hair
radiated beams of light through my skull
and into my brain
to enlighten my soul
the hands that gifted me
my very first prayer book
that made me fall in love
with spirituality
the hands that i held
tightly asking the universe
why you had to leave
while you lay
in your casket
they were still warm
i know you
will be with me
until we meet again
i look forward to holding
your warm hands
once again

until i see you again

"sab abhi nicalo" ("everybody out now")
he heard this unnerving demand
and froze
he dropped his plate full of roti
a race
to make the last train out of the village
the train before him slain
neighbors
friends
classmates
uncles
aunts
mother and father
as the sun rose
the train came to a halt
to a village of tents
lined for miles and miles
his new home
a young orphan
refugee

india-pakistan partition

when i rest my head
on your soft shoulder
i feel that everything
is going to be alright
when i wrap my lanky arms
around you
i feel your heart beating
gently
it calms my heart
a warmth that i feel
only with you
you have always cheered me on
from very front of the bleachers
as a child
raising me into the air
above your
amazonian
five foot nine frame
gazing at me in admiration
with your
piercing green eyes
to tell me how strong
of a woman i will grow up to be
even when i was too young to understand
but i felt it
ever since
you held me in your arms
i have felt that
i am in the presence
of a goddess
i have been raised
by a king

dear mother

my mother and father
came to this country
from a small gem
nestled in northwestern india
called punjab
where the milk and butter
are served fresh daily
where you will find
the most green grass
out of all the lands
where everyone is treated
like celestial beings
where the food
makes your taste buds
run wild
my parents left their land
for the western world
they gave up
security for uncertainty
they gave up their education
to give my brother and i an education
they gave up a beautiful home
to scrape by to make rent each month
they gave up
their sense of belonging
in their homeland
for a chance to fit in…

...in a new world
where they were welcomed with open arms
to be labeled as aliens
rather than akin
struggling to fit in
when they wanted them
to fit out
but with time
the new world
slowly became home
with spices
and teas
stocked up in cabinets
to ease the nostalgia
just a little bit

punjabi immigrants

to the man who threw
a half eaten apple
at my grandfather
for wearing a turban
although i was still in my mom's belly
my first instinct
would be to tell you off
but then
i realize
that your parochial mind
has probably been passed on
from your mother and father
and their mother and father
your hatred is not your fault
it is what you were watered
when you were a seed underneath
the earth's soil
at breakfast
your brain was fed
how to judge people who do not look like you
at lunch
your eyes were shown
the labels to paste on people who do not look like you
at dinner
your body was taught
how to react towards people who do not look like you
you had the liberation
of changing your meal plan
when you became a man
but the heartbreaking part is
you continue to choose
the same dishes

his mother's menu

the turban
is rewarded
after great sacrifices
have been made
the turban
is the gift from the guru
it represents
equality among all people
of all colors and all faiths
it is a promise
to prove our faith in god by
serving the impoverished
and lifting them up
it is a promise
to take the presence of the guru
wherever we go
it is the symbol of
a warrior
it is a promise
to protect those who cannot
protect themselves

the sikh turban

to be an american is to
wear a burka
a turban
or a warbonnet
and feel safe
it is to be able to
walk into a shop
wearing a saree
a kimono
or a sarape
and not be bothered
about people looking at you strange
it is to openly speak
spanish
punjabi
hindi
farsi
arabic
tagalog
mandarin
korean
or any of the other beautiful
languages from all over the world
and not be fearful of people
treating you as inferior
america can wear a burka
speak spanish and gracefully dance
kathak
america can wear a turban
practice sikhism and speak
tagalog
america is a beautiful clay vase
made from the soil of *every* country

a colorful america

every night before bed
my mother
whispered in my ear
that my mind
is a diamond
my heart
is gold
before ever calling me beautiful
she engraved in me
the importance
of having a beautiful mind
and an empathetic heart
something that
far transcends
outer beauty

ingredients of a pretty soul

to this day
when the women of rural india
verbally stand up for themselves
and their daughters
some men are quick
to put a finger in front of her lips
shoving her beautiful voice
back into her mouth
the thoughts that would have
bolted out
to dance around in her daughter's ears
and make her smile
he looks at her
with such depreciating eyes
that she does not dare open
the padlock
of the closet
she put her words back into
within the deepest corner of her mind

village secrets

every time
they leave their little girl
on the street
an angel dies
at the sound of the baby girl
crying
but then
that angel is reborn
within that little girl
and she finds
the courage
to collect herself
she waters her own seeds
and blooms the most
resilient flower
that no gust of wind
could knock down

female feticide: save the girl

the sound of nitnem prayers
the smell of fresh chai
and a ray of light
shining through my pie
shaped window
blessed my eyes
my nose
and my ears
every morning
i rushed downstairs
to embrace my nanaji
beads in hand
"*waheguru*"
next bead
"*waheguru*"
next bead
lost in
the inner cosmos

sublime mornings

'*tu tere ghar hi jaana*'
these five words
are engraved
in the minds of
little girls
in rural india
since birth
her rights cut off
along with the umbilical cord
treated like an outsider
since childhood
because after all
as they say
"*you are going
to get married off
and go away
to your husband's home*"
she is told
that that is her home
that she can only
spread her wings
when she has departed
her birth home

her life begins in her mother's belly

school
market
home
school
market
home
he had her daily routine
memorized
worshipping her from behind
the chaiwala shop
adoring her
spidery long legs
and flawless black hair
the young beauty
came home
with not one spot
on her face
that did not screech
of abuse
the boy walked home
grinning ear to ear
the entire village
condemned the girl
"it is your fault
your legs
were on display"

rape in india

tucked away
in the hills of haryana
mother and father
sit quietly
the nerves so tense
you could hear
their daughter's tears
escaping her
big almond eyes
she wanted to
become an attorney
her parents wanted
her to marry
but their small dowry
said otherwise
she was not
playing competitively
in the marriage market
"what was the use"
the father said
"in creating you
if no one will marry you
nobody wants
a poor man's daughter"
the tragedy was
they failed to see
how beautiful
her soul really was
one that no endowment
could measure up to

the dowry

there she lay
on the spa bed
counting the tiles on the roof
there were 40
as the white cream
excruciatingly
seeped into her skin
washing her dusky glow
each time she reached
for the water to wash her face
the television ad broadcasted
loud and clear
"beauty is pain
after this
you will be fair
and lovely"
forcing her head back down
then
she could marry up
the thought
of never being looked down on
for her
dark complexion
made her happy
so she powered through
the pain
she just wanted
to be pretty for them
she just wanted
their acceptance

dark and lovely

outside the bazaar
the little girl who called the
dirt road her home
threw her apprehensive eyes
at me
but before they shied away
i smiled
then she smiled
i pressed my hands
together
and brought them
to the center of my soul
and bowed
"*namasté*"
she did the same
"*namaste didi*"
i bought her
her favorite meal
we sat and we ate
together
she put her last
piece of naan
in her pocket
and skipped away
to feed another child
who also lived
down the dirt road

humanity has no caste

i am away from my home
but i am
home
with my ancestors
i throw the curtains open
and the warmth
of the mid-december sun
caresses my face
i step out onto the balcony
the warmth
of the marble floors
never felt so comforting
i reach north
to the blue skies
then east
towards
acres and acres
of the greenest grass
the swiss grass
of the far east
as they say
the sweet sound
of peacocks from the west
and my grandmother
calling me from south
for some fresh aloo paranthas
and home made yogurt

samrai: my father's village

i saw a tall man
seated
on the turquoise park bench
both arms resting on
his walking cane
his long white beard
moving liberally with the wind
his grey eyes on an excursion
looking past the mountains
they squint to focus
widen in discovery
then come back to their
resting place
enthusiastically
sharing his journeys
with me
the cherry blossom trees
in japan
dancing fandango under the
spanish sun
playing holi to ring in spring time
in india
i ask him how
he points to his mind
'in here my child'

imaginative escapades

the reds
of purity and bravery
the oranges
of courage and sacrifice
the blues
of immortality and resilience
the greens
of harvest and happiness
fold into your own nest
to keep you warm
on colder days

my great grandmother's shawls

the laughing faces
of the people
i love the most
blithe and jovial
we have forgotten
of the rough patches
from the past
the stories
being washed down
with hot chai tea
beating the frigid
winter nights
with a few blankets
tucked under our toes
in the middle of all
this elation
i took around and observe
the happiness
each person brings
into my life
knowing that
we will never be here
in this moment
on this very day
again
the nostalgia
takes a front seat
i already miss now

family

with turquoise tasseled
prayer beads in hand
i can feel your spirit
running through
my veins
as soon as
i pick them up
i can hear the
17 years
of wisdom
you left me with
before you walked
down toward the green
exit sign
and then you turned back
to give me one last glace
to gift me
your most precious
turquoise tasseled
prayer beads
before turning the corner
to join
the eternal power

nanaji

the call for
her vertebral deterioration
came at 4am
when she rose
to sew the spines
of the leather notebooks
for the boys to use
with their textbooks

school dreams

iqbal singh samra

resting my head on your shoulder
was the best medicine
money cannot buy
a sense of comfort and warmth
rushed into my bloodstream
in that moment i knew i would be alright
because you were with me
your organs were frowning but
there was nothing but light
radiating through your heart
why couldn't this light
have turned everything around
to good health for you
i ask the creator
when my heart would fall down
a cliff there you would be sitting
at the foot of my bed knowing without
spoken word that something was wrong
and would make me smile again
with one of your dad jokes
you reassured me that i am
a woman made of steel
you made sure i knew
that i must go to battle to get what i want
in this life
although it kills me that i cannot rest
my head on your shoulder until i join you
in heaven
i do not feel your absence in my heart
i know you are here with me
and you always will be
afterall you are my blood
i am proudly your daughter
for eternity

papa

they burst through the front door
like the tears hurriedly
racing down their faces
desperate to find comfort
embracing mom
brother and myself
their hugs offer
momentary comfort
silence
as we absorb the emptiness
in the room
they look at me
pity broadcasted on their faces
but why?
he is with god
so his blessings will be 10 fold
i look forward to him being
a grandfather
and watching his grandchildren
grow
i look at you and smile
"papa is with me"
as i wipe away
the tears underneath
your eyes
he does not want to see
you cry

future nanaji

the aroma of peppered omelets
makes me jump out of bed
the chilly morning air
does not trouble me
for i am excited for breakfast
i open my door
greeted by *"come eat kiddo"*
the omelets
perfectly lining
the circumference of the plate
cut into four pieces
cooked well done
just as i've liked my eggs
since i was four
papa patiently waits
with his arms crossed
and eyes closed
for the toaster
to shoot the bread into the sky
there it goes!
lovingly placing it on the plate
making sure mom and i
have everything we need
before taking his seat
at the head of the table

breakfast with papa

i take a bite of my toast
and as it struggles
to pass down my throat
my eyes fill up with water
my head
throbbing
my stomach
in knots
i hear
"*come eat kiddo*"
and i look over
to an empty kitchen
the pots and pans
are perfectly clean
right where i left them
the table is empty
and the aroma is
deceased
the toaster is untouched
and the egg carton is full
but
you *just* called me
to breakfast

breakfast without papa

i wake up
in a cold sweat
panicking
an abduction has occurred
have you seen my dad?
he stands six feet tall
a handsome tan man
with beautiful hazel eyes
and brown hair
i squeeze toothpaste onto my brush
my breathing heavy
i still do not know where he is
i grasp my countertop and close my eyes
his face and a million memories
flash before my eyes
hello? are you there? papa?
are you ok? i open my eyes
and burst open the bathroom doors
i open your closet
there are your clothes
untouched for a month now
just as you left them
they are sitting there waiting to be worn
for god's sake come back and wear them!
i scroll through the photos on my phone
the last one from july 25, 2019
three days before you were taken
to the hospital
how can this be? how can i talk to you papa?
how can i reach you? maybe if i called you
so i do
one ring
two rings
three rings
voicemail

desperate to hear your comforting voice
i listen to the most recent
voicemail you left me
on july 27, 2019
my heart races faster and faster
as my thumb reaches the play button
a strong calming voice
"kid, come pick me up from the hospital
i'm ready to go"
my body freezes
i'm coming papa
i'm coming!
i get into my car
my mom stops me
"where are you going dear"
i say
"to get dad
he needs me
he wants to come home"
mom looks at me
and points at the sun peaking through
the puffy sunday morning
clouds
"he is home dear"

searching for you

its been a while
since i heard your voice
its been a while
since we had our morning
and evening cup of chai
together
we have not talked about
poetry in quite some time
i have not listened to
kanwar grewal yet
because we have
to do that together
i'm sitting here
waiting at my desk
for you to come in any minute
with tea
so we can talk about our days
i look at the door cracked open
still hoping you will step in
at any moment
smiling
i look at your watch
it has been two months since you last
looked at it

it's been so long

how is it papa?
up there
where i imagine the oxygen is as crisp
as an october morning
and the air smells like fresh linen
on a sunday
have you seen grandpa yet?
how is he?
tell him i still have his
turquoise tassel prayer beads
and i use them to pray
every morning and evening
how is the food?
remember
do not eat too much sugar
you are a diabetic!
i cut back on my tea
it is just not the same
when you are up there
and i am here
i miss calling you on my lunch break
to talk about the most random things
and cracking jokes
you smiled before
you went up there to god
do you remember that?
your face was shining
and you pointed to the sky
i can only imagine how happy
you are
i look forward to the day
we meet again
we will have tea

a letter to my father

your last breath has escaped
my knees have given out
my head pounding
from the pain of your departure
but
i fake my strength
for my mother and brother
i feel your hand on my shoulder
mending back my frail spirit
momentarily
whispering in my ear
that you are always with me
you encourage us not to cry
as you are finally free of pain
as the rest of the family gathers
you watch us from above
joyous that we have come together
to reflect how wonderful of a person
you are
when i close my eyes to rest
i see your smiling face
and it breaks my heart
knowing that when i open my eyes
you will not be there
but then i remember
you have relocated
to a permanent home
in my heart

forever with me

today
it hurts a little extra
i am at the dip
of the roller coaster
when i opened my eyes
this morning
i was desperate to find you
to smell the chai you made me
every morning
my heart falls down a well
a well
thousands of feet deep
a well so deep into the earth
that retrieving it
is an impossible task
i feel as if
i will vomit up my insides
where will i see you again?
will i see you roaming the fields
of punjab
that you so arduously worked in
to support your family
when your own father passed away?
will i see you peacefully soaking in
the beauty of the snowcapped
cascade mountains in your
favorite state of oregon?
i breathe deeply
and a warm brush on my shoulder
is that you papa?
another warm brush on my shoulder
yes
it is you

hello again

your hazel eyes
peak down
at your tan wrist
complimented by
a rustic silver watch
your everyday watch
tick
tock
tick
tock
you watch the dial
move timidly towards 12
to complete the hour
with the patience of a saint
and a smirk on your face
sometimes the dials are silver
for everyday use
sometimes gold
for special occasions
sometimes copper
for everyday use
when you get tired of the silver one
the feeling of punctuality
and owning time
when the links click together
you peer out
into the california sun
with that chunky weight
on your left wrist
and smile once again
as you cross your arms
looking into the distance
proudly knowing
that you are indeed
the master of time

my father's watches

you taught me how to change the car oil
you taught me how to drive
you instilled in me
the power of hard work
the importance of honesty
and generosity
as a child when i fell and scraped
my knees
you told me to get up
and dust myself off
when i finished my homework
you gave me extra books to read
you taught me how to pray
with my hands pressed together
at the center of my being
you made sure i knew
that there is nothing in this life
that i cannot accomplish
you showed me
relentless work ethic
the importance of persistence
and perseverance
determination
and will power
how to keep my composure in tough times
and how to propel through them
and before you departed this earth
you made sure i knew
the importance of being a strong woman
and standing on my own feet
so firmly that no hurricane
could ever knock me down

thank you, papa

i open your bedroom door
a gust of icy air
to the left your favorite part
of the room
your work desk
there are your set of keys
just as you left them
two keys waiting to be put on a ring
you were in the middle of
making a set of keys
your pen had just finished
writing a sentence in
your bills binder
its sitting there
waiting for you to write with it
your night pajamas hung behind the door
and one shirt on the floor
there are
your set of pens that
you were in the middle of organizing
your prayer book unwrapped
you had just finished praying
but didn't get a chance to put
it back in it's resting cloth
in your bathroom
the baby blue towel
you used to wipe your face
after you washed it
as you were feeling ill
crunched up on the countertop
it has been 18 days
your things miss you

coming home after papa passed

i will share with the world
how wonderful of a father you are
where do i start?
these pages just do not suffice
when i was three
you watched me climb up the house tree
always there to catch me
with those long strong arms
the garden you so lovingly planted for us
with fresh strawberries and blueberries
wild berries and blackberries
red beats and beat red tomatoes
lettuce and carrots
artichoke and spinach
waking up at five to shovel the snow
out of the drive
to get to school on time
so my mind could thrive
you watered the seeds of my mind
and let it grow a forest
not once clipping the branches or leaves
on that frightening snowy california night
you pulled me out of our crushed car
and saved my life
under the starry december night
crying uncontrollably
but my superhero father saved me
softening my sobbing
your mind spilling with knowledge
the theology philosophy business and law
that i learned from you…

…could fill an entire bookshelf wall
the kind you need one of those
rolling wooden ladders for
the delicious indian food you would cook
that filled the room with the aroma of our motherland
your love of stationary
the furry winter hat that you refused to remove
even in the middle of june
sometimes you swapped it with your
summer baseball cap
as you looked at your maps
and squeezed in a catnap
basking in the california sun
your love of tracking time
by the watches that shine
strapped around your wrist
making sure you never
missed being top of the line
your love of soaps and washing your hands
when i asked for something
one was not enough
you would buy me double and sometimes triple
and whenever my spirit was low
you would give me a nudge
with your elbow
and a little memo
that hey
after a storm comes a rainbow
with the most comforting smile
waking up at dawn
to call on me and mom
that tea and breakfast
is ready

and when things went south
in the recession
so did your health
many let us down
using their hands to point fingers
rather than lift
people at our doorstep
when were well
not one soul
when we were not
i quickly learned how the world works
you continued to keep your chin up
powering through the hurtful words
i will never forget
the emotional pain
they inflicted on you
i could see it in your hazel eyes
that was the first time
i saw you cry
our family road trips down the five
as i soaked in the beauty
of the drive
you took the wheel
singing along ghazals
on my road trips home from college
you called me every hour
to see where i was
so you could cook for me
my favorite indian food
your knowledge of
our beautiful punjabi culture
that made me want to
nosedive
deep into our roots
to share it with

the rest of the world
you taught me
the true meaning of wealth
lifting people up out of adversity
selflessly serving the poor
and knowledge
not what lies in our wallets
and bank accounts
one day when i too die
i hope to leave this world
half of the incredible human being
that you are
to join you
in the highest part
of the astral world

sardar iqbal singh samra

lately
dreams have been heavenly
and reality has been a nightmare
when i close my eyes
i hope it is
a one way ticket
rather than a round trip
to dreamland
i see your comforting face
you tell me that you are no longer ill
that you are free and fine
we play fetch with the dog
we have tea and talk about the universe
like old times
you spill out knowledge until you get
tired and excuse yourself for bed time
i open my eyes in our new home
where i can go to mom's room
and open your side of the closet
but your things are
not there
i thought you had come back

sweet dreams

kidnap me from this
nightmare that is my reality
let me sleep some more
so i may bask in my dreams
the only place where
i can find you

a living nightmare

the birth of their steel backs

in this day and age
the volume of perishable things
subdue
a crystalline heart
and a mind that dazzles

society

a loud fire cracker
darren's body numb
but he had to act fast
if he wanted to stay alive
a vague memory of the drill the teachers
had shown him
"get down and hide!"
he collapsed onto the floor
and buried himself under desks
he heard the door crash open
desks flipping over
and footsteps
a screech
not just any screech
one that desperately pleaded to be spared
but an undertone of hopelessness
another screech another firework
another screech another firework
footsteps
growing closer and closer
silence
the combat boots paused
for what seemed like an hour
now
facing the barricade of desks
darren was hiding under
the voice of the devil himself
"anybody here"
an era long pause
"come out and i won't hurt you"
as he snickered
a ping from the pile of desks beside him
the shooter threw the barricade of desks up...

...a screech and a firework
darren froze into an icicle
as a stream of blood
hurriedly traveled to his knees

school shootings

she smiled
she could feel the mist on her skin
she could hear the water
hurriedly cascading down the jade cliffs
as if quenching
the thirst of the boulders below
as if
quenching her own
she woke
the edges of her mouth
cracking
her throat crusty
a train had just struck her brain
her eyes pleading to close
so they could rest
they widened and bolted
left to right
the waterfall had vanished
her heavy eyes adamantly closed
and there it was again
tall and grand
crashing down
the cliffside

a lush waterfall

the sun sizzled his back
each hour depositing .50 cents in his pocket
just as the threw his shovel down
his daughter's voice
played in his head
she wants books to read
and notebooks to write in for school
there had to be food on the table
to feed his wife and the bundle of joy
growing inside of her
three were about to become four
he thought of returning
to his motherland
back to a broken government
back to a home made of mud
and plastic
back to a home in the slums
where his daughter's voice
would be trapped behind
her sewn lips
just as they got off the boat
so he picked up the shovel
on second thought
the hot sun
was not so bad afterall

the undercooked american dream

scoop
toss back
scoop
toss back
the tractor passed by him
and started a little dust storm
as he took a breath
and pulled his shovel back
to attack the next pile of dirt
teeny tiny particles
unseen by the eye
bolted into his body
dashing down to his lungs
there they spread
like wildfire
a little fever
a cough here
a cough there
first went his breath
then his kidneys
then his heart
then
his life

valley fever

for the children i am a tree
i grow tall and grand to bear fruit
to feed the hungry ones and shade their backs
protecting them from the sweltering summer sun
i give comfort to the children so they can
rest on my trunk and read
in the pursuit of creating libraries in their minds
i give branches so they can use them
for fire on cold days
i give them a jungle gym to swing and climb
to sit on and watch the sun go away
for the day
behind the mountains
of the wild west

the altruist

he painted the redwoods of california
the snow-capped peaks of everest
the crystal blue waters of the maldives
the floral blooms of maharastra
but you chose to have no sight
when he grew weak and his hands gave in
you demanded the greatest piece
and broadcasted his inability to grip a paintbrush

protect your truth

a beautiful sunny
december day at the bazaar
the stranger threw her a smile
she smiled back
the next day he gave her a smile again
her face grew red her eyes shuffled left to right
she reciprocated out of fear
a smile was not an invitation
but to him it was
the man approached her and grabbed her hand
"*choro*" ("*let me go*") she said hesitantly
she pushed him away
then
a sudden splash
engulfed her beautiful face
her skin boiling
as she collapsed to the floor

acid attacks

her mind was hungry
she wanted the privilege
to feed it
to break the lineage
of women who have
sealed their hopes
and dreams
in a box
and shelved it
at the top corner
of the pantry

paperback mind meals

he unclenched his fist
a few peanuts and raisins
that were his
three course meal
his chocolate brown eyes
peeked through the window
droplets of the november rain
dampening his raven hair
he zipped up the window
and buried his face
in the pillow
his tummy grew hollow
as he rested
on the frigid concrete
beneath his bones
that he called
home

skid row